SUEŃO DEL ALMA:
22 ANDALUSIAN SONNETS

Cat Woodward was born in Lancashire in 1990. Cat holds a PhD in lyric poetics from the University of East Anglia. In 2018 she won the Ivan Juritz Prize for Creative Experiment. Cat mentors and teaches Creative Writing. Her full length collection *Strange Shape* (Gatehouse, 2024) was shortlisted for The East Anglian Book Awards 2024.

Also by Cat Woodward

Strange Shape   (Gatehouse, 2024)

Blood, Flower, Joy!   (Knives, Forks and Spoons, 2019)

Sphinx   (Salò, 2017)

CONTENTS

ISBN: 978-1-916938-73-1

The author has asserted their right to be identified as the author of this Work in accordance with the Copyright, Designs and Patents Act 1988

Cover designed by Aaron Kent

Edited and Typeset by Aaron Kent

Broken Sleep Books Ltd
PO BOX 102
Llandysul
SA44 9BG

Sueño del Alma

Cat Woodward

Broken Sleep Books

I dreamt that several bougainvilleas after the
bougainvillea, deep inside the bougainvillea,
behind an orange petal: the real Bougainvillea.
Apricot Bougainvilleas cover a house whose

cool marble stair I'm descending; the dead
in their neighbouring apartments laugh, make
love, learn to play their instruments. I hear
the wrought banister's roughness comment

to the smoothness of the tile: *the House of*
Dream has bouquets and vases, but no scent.
In the parched courtyard is a gate and beyond it

the street, where I see, dissected by the iron
grille, myself. I am shabby, without prologue,
nose to the dust, out there sniffing like a dog.

Enormous yellow hill, the yellow of cymbals
and loud brass instruments; my gaze peels
the skin off you like the rind of a grapefruit.
And you, sea, full of those relentless spiritual

boulders that roll in things, how you hurl your
blue soul at my finely-whetted eyes. A coast
reflects the agonies of heaven, returning the
diligent stare with its own little fleck of god.

Soon, the sun melts the yellow hill to a pool
of stippled gold, the sea dries to a lid of salt,
the boulders go back in the angels' pockets,

and I am recalled into that dreadful passion
while, anchored to the air as by a sturdy hook,
all that remains is my look.

Already the stars are sinking, which were rising
when I set out; here the bald river rocks, like
dinosaur eggs, or human skulls, scatter and knock
against my horse's hoof; the blood-drop moon

turns red as any rust. What can it be, hatching
within me, that its searching, squirming finger
calls, infantile, to a larger sea? And this dry
channel, with its rising smoke of dust, conveys

me firmly, like a penny in a slot? I can smell it,
odorous as the fox, oyster quiet, luxuriant
as locks: first frog, then snake, shark, then ox.

O changeling Future, leaking queerly, I delayed
once, now I ride with grave, ponderous motion
and with skittering steps toward that ocean.

Poet, I saw you there under the white sun,
standing in red dust, so still, as if you were
fired there like glass. I saw your stare, a radial
from the tense centre of your will.

There, fixed by that point, I saw your subject,
as filled with its image as a bull with breath, a hot
brute with lowered head, and between you the deep
line it was gouging powerfully in the dirt.

Then, snapping, some florid eyelid within you lifted
and against that thin flutter your subject rushed
with the full force of its smoking, snorting soul.

Revolving then inside your poem, its dreaming
look rose up like a bubble from a boiling pot;
the struck bullseye, seeing you, recognised what?

Blue! Lead-dense. Blue, that vast wing curving
far beyond the little circumference of the eye.
Blue, that blue dagger-point puncturing, or blue,
that hot coal blue, diffusing to ultimate extent.

Blue laps carefully the coastlines of us smaller
forms, rounding us soft as glass in its wave.
Exterior without interior, without back to turn
away from my sweating, shaded view. Blue,

with hard look, persuades subtleness into flesh.
Blue covers me, soaking into me the colour of
open gates. O Blue, from the giant horizon

I hear your imploring: *you there! Yes, you!*
Turn slightly (that's right, just so)
dissolve into drops now! Evaporate, go!

From that mauve horizon girdling the visible, perfected
Future washes in, comes rolling up through all its
pandemonious depth, to break upon a coastline
as this present moment's off-white foam. Starlight,

ploughing its eons straight down, makes a final
flourish and bursts from the tree as a green leaf;
meanwhile, the warmth of night works its designs
on me, transforming suddenly into my sigh. Here,

my thoughts wait, divided from some great arrival,
prickling as if they felt a hand on the other side of
the air. My thoughts, curled close around that dark

lugubrious thing called a heart, feel a fullness melt
them, melt them into unrecognisable emanations,
which fullness then receives with silent ministrations.

Back to back with myself in the quiet of my bed,
I cling to her like honey to a spoon or like shadow
to the sole of a foot. Why not turn to look at me?
Why not catch me in the act? The droplets which

clung to the arms of Narcissus, clung no less jealously
than I. If nothing is wounding me, then why am I
kept open as though I expected someone to enter
and turn on all the lights? Who then slipped a cold

mirror between her and I, distinctly perceptible
at the shoulder? As a glove suggests a hand, I am
suggesting her quietly, all night long. All night I am

turning my head to look. Myself, have you felt
my hot eye skirting your solid temple? Have you
dreamt you felt a small, mute itching, have you?

A parasol extends its coloured palm and
the noon sun puts down its coin to say *soon,
but not now*. A white ball, having been thrown
cringes at the top of its arc, while below the

watching sand asks *when?* Inside my glass,
ice is circled by patient Heat, *not yet* it squeaks,
while the tall crests of the boisterous sea
break loudly into a single: *almost*! In the shade

I wait stupidly, the way a breadcrumb waits
to be snatched by the expressionless sparrow.
Cicadas are deciding what to tell their small god.

High up in a Spanish pine squats the dead man,
he leans out, peering like a crusty old bird.
Have you heard? he asks, *I've heard.*

Solitude: the terrible vocation. One's voice
sounding inside oneself, a dog whistle,
the hard gem of the soul cultivating grain by
grain in darkness. Who did you expect to meet

in that enormity, wandering as you do for
hours? Down here you are like the blind eye
of a too distant star. No place for seeing, this,
where privacy gestates something like the

full, dumb tongues of grapes. What is fruiting
inside you, and with such agony and so little
consolation? What shapes do your moving lips

make, you who are lost the way only children
can be lost, cleaving to a vast, sudden fracture
which precisely fits their tiny stature?

Implacable clarity of ice. The eyes dive through like
a streak of oil, seize the nude heart and see
nothing. Clear ice, like the phantom in the corner
of a child's room.

What brilliant diamond is daily, nightly, held against
my illiterate sight? And what invisible wind cradles
this slack chin? If my vision should pause as it passed
through such clearness, how cold it would be, frozen

there astounded, as by the moon or a breast bared
suddenly; the implicit spectre sitting inside my flesh
as in a chair might bristle to feel invisible kin.

But, dead ahead the eye's unerring arrow
flies, through sheerness sheerer than chiffon,
piercing all, piercing on and on and on and on.

Night, count your olives, count what is yours
and allowed to go with you. The dead woman
in the olive orchard stoops to pick up a paper
plate. She has been quietly filling our house

with her smell. Night, give me rest from the
dead woman, her corpse on our table is still
brown with the dirt we threw in after her,
as I watch she wipes her face. Night, let me

not feel the dead woman, whose tongue we
stole when we buried it under a tombstone.
From the door, the dead woman looks out at

me, enraged. Count me among those things
that are made safe in your purse, and so live.
No, not you, you are a black, too bitter olive.

My grandfather died in my throat, my tongue
kept him safe. I said *family*; you did not say *family*.
I waited for the time when I would not be alone.
It was you who refilled my cup, which I drank

in silence. Even my chair was budding. Spring
drove his plough over me and laughed handsomely.
You did not laugh. I thought I felt my grandmother's
hand, but it was only you combing my hair. A razor

could not be induced between my teeth. You said,
your grandfather's corpse has been misplaced, and
knowing slipped under my door like a dish. I spoke;

you answered not like a husband to a wife.
You were saying your shibboleth,
O Angel of Death.

Air baked white as salt, or white like a dry and silent
bone. The burning months are this: a too long pause
that shrivels the mouth and stupefies the tongue.
We shrink, bellies to the grit, and are like tuning forks

yet to be struck.   Then,
guitar notes, notes of rain; guitar notes falling,
falling like tears, like stars, like seeds. The leaf opens
her little ear, as does the wine cup, the roof tile, to hear

music cascading from her neighbours. Everywhere,
castanets. The guitar, silver-green, melodious, is singing
in a clear, light voice that steers through the pines,

is singing to the roof tile, to the wine cup, to the leaf,
and to the woman in the house, and the egg in the nest:
Go in now, go in and rest.

Euphorbia milii
Corona de Cristo, Thorns of Christ

Thumb sprouted from yellow rock, all brawn
and blush. Fiesta cockspur; frilly cuff. Lip of flesh;
tiger's head. Lamb skinned and tilted to the sky's blue
bell. Cockatiel. Flinty garnet chips. Hands, spread.

How each eye beam, landing on your image's
griddle, sizzles! And also, how the air beside you
scintillates, as though it felt a prodigious heat! I watch
your thorn, caught on Time's passing skirt, unseam it!

How you humble her, as she runs by you, naked!
And how my spirit, entered now by yours, pops
like a bud, or a burning blood sausage into that

self-same red. But then, at the sound of 'Lunch!'
or 'My love?', the tinted lens withdraws its power,
and I see by the pool, a tight-lipped, crafty flower.

The moon comes swishing her silk skirt,
changing all the locks, comes flinging wide
the windows I had so covetously shut. Loose
drapes blow ingress into the huge, hot night.

And on the other side of a strip of air: exit.
And everywhere, always, those who are exiting,
who go dipping their toes tentatively, daintily,
into loyal hereafter. The moon comes, urging

egress; she is so like a lover in a play, returned
to my window with her jewels and jasmine perfume,
comehithering. But wait, who then is entering,

foot on sash? Tentatively, daintily?
A familiar shoe, so familiar is its shade and line,
and in its worn suppleness, how very like mine.

Eleven illuminations of the soul: the shadow of a
face falls on a white tablecloth among jamón and
croquetas; a hairy hand stretches cling film across

a new tattoo of a heart; black ribbon unspools behind
a wooden boat, a gale blows; a bowling ball diving
furiously down through the sea; a gecko scuttles by a
vase of scented paper flowers, the room is cool, dark;

a slow, shallow river pawing at a rock like a dog; slowly,
ochre dust is cleaned off a tile by rain; the reflection
of the moon lands in a glass of yellow wine; one of

several knots in a string, a charm for binding love;
orange begonias on the porch at night: above, stars;
distantly, music of the accordion, smoke of cigars.

Turning, the rim of a carriage wheel describes
a nut-brown arc. So the sun drops sharply and,
copper-coloured, declines through this poem,
heavy as the falling tongue of a bell. Sun falls

into a forest, as if it were a spent pine needle
that could be hidden by the rest. A hand might
hold that sun as it might a tan egg, or a lemon
cast in bronze. Sun slips on through the poem,

and with a luminous finger, gilds the earthworm,
commands the caterpillar moth. At that spot, the
soil turns red as cloth. But then comes Night who,

rolling back her inky sleeve, crouches down and
covers that strange ember with her silent thumb.
In the dark it rises weightless, back where it had come.

Specks of time, like pimento seeds, or like a
child's nail clippings, come filing in singly. They rise
up as from a dark ocean the colour of cassis, but
pass through one's pockets just like breadcrumbs

or last year's sand. If I were to obliterate the office
clock, what angel would congratulate me? What
moment would cling to me still, like a stray grain
of saffron-coloured rice? Rain streaks the golden

lamps of the street just as well as it does the golden
lamps of the heart. But the heart can stroke what
passes by it, if it likes. Listen to that old god there,

twanging his lyre, sprouting obnoxious little ears
on the lot. I'll tell you the secret of his mischance:
when Orpheus looked back, he only glanced.

Surely, you've seen him, my man. His broad back
shines through his clothes. His bare hand holds
the sun in harness; he reins then rides the truculent
Spring, his male soul following like wood smoke

where he goes. Surely you saw him, panting, leading
the flowers back out from soil's long, dark dream,
then kindling their little lights in millions. Tell me
you've seen this man, whose gold shoulders

glow through even the most tightly closed eyelids.
Where he points his thumb, things know what they ought
to become, and non-things what they now must be.

If you see him, you'll surely know him, for when
he passes, each stone he passes cries after him, loudly:
love me, love me, love me, love me!

Red rose at night: awake now, she is speaking
only to herself. She raises her voice to barely
the volume of a fragrance, and you? You stop,
turn back, and spied on by the prying little stars,

attend to her. Image, that salamander unburned
by the fires of the Looking, emerges again from
invisible cinders, then bolting it scurries a trail
through its own spent ash. It is gone. All these

ashes of the Looking blow, scatter, precede us
into the earth. But Image? There it goes, whole
and burnished again by the eye's live fires. And

you there, you still hold the rose, fresh and red.
You picture such things as though once caught,
you might divide even the rose from her thought.

A nightingale sings from a gravestone, his song
is the core around which a year grows, each one
adding its annual ring. And the dead, from some
likewise sympathy with roots and stars, thicken

here to keep their secrets warm. I imagine (or I
anticipate) divesting, bequeathing myself to the
flowers and to the mushrooms' furtive kind who,
in their blooming, part the lush hairs of grass; not

Life, not Thought, but some other limpid fire, this
amphibious, lustrous albumin that rests itself like
a moonbeam on a log; I imagine this pendulous

filament hanging from its source: two paired
effulgences, who each in the other confide
and whom neither height nor depth can divide.

In the flower, it is felt as the dream of fruit;
daily, that terrible ripening of the soul. Death
crouches within you like any stone, until
grown and ungreen you are gathered,

my Love: gathered your shirt and your shoes,
gathered your hands, your feet, your hair, your
disappointments all gathered, with your sleeping,
your coat, your comb; and gathered my neck,

my thighs, my dress, my impatience gathered,
gathered my love, my nails, my rings, my whole
garden gathered; and our pockets, our minutes,

our pillows and mattress, our kisses all gathered in.
O Love, Autumn comes and brings in all it can bring,
then after Autumn, Winter. But after Winter, Spring.

ACKNOWLEDGEMENTS

With thanks to Flo, whose help in sequencing this pamphlet was invaluable.

LAY OUT YOUR UNREST